I am

An identity affirming colouring book.

I Am: An identity affirming colouring book

Series: Mindful colouring

© C.R. Draper, 2023

'All rights reserved. No part of this book may be reproduced in any form or by any electronic or mechanical means, without permission in writing from the copyright owner.

ISBN: 978-1-922819-03-1

I can do difficult things

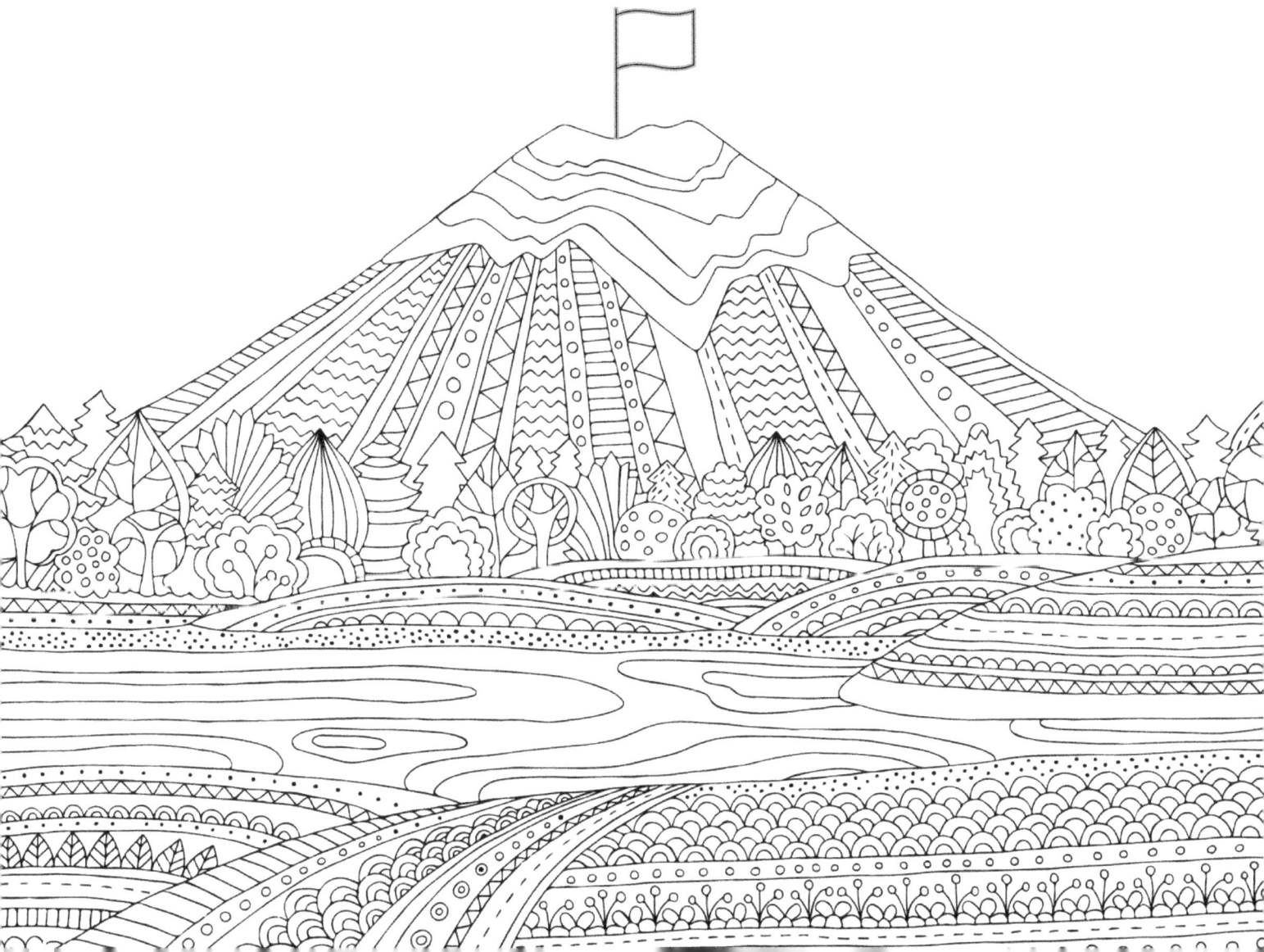

I am confident

I am free to
be myself

I learn from my mistakes

I stand up for what I believe in

I am patient

I can try again

I can learn new things

I can persevere

www.ingramcontent.com/pod-product-compliance
Lightning Source LLC
Chambersburg PA
CBHW051319110526
44590CB00031B/4402